If Only

Poems by

Josh Slotnick

Sandyhouse Press

IF ONLY

For information, contact:
Sandyhouse Press
163408 Hollirob Lane
Wausau, WI, 54403

Published in the United States of America

ISBN: 978-0-9833110-8-9
Library of Congress Control Number: 2023909215

Cover art by Quinn Slotnick-Murchison
Design and layout by Jamie Tipton, Open Heart Designs

For Steve and Luci,
If not for you, I wouldn't have believed it possible.

Contents

AWAY   47

SKINNY OLIVE-SKINNED JEW BOY ON THE HIGH PLAINS GETS MISTAKEN FOR MEXICAN, IRANIAN, LIVES IN RURAL SOUTH-EAST ASIA, SPEAKS THE LANGUAGE, GROWS UP TO BE A MIDDLE-CLASS WHITE GUY IN MONTANA AND OVER A PERIOD OF YEARS INADVERTANTLY WRITES A FEW POEMS FROM THIS LIMITED PERSPECTIVE   69

POEMS TO   77

Preface

*J*osh Slotnick *is a father and a farmer, a teacher and a traveler.*
Curiously he somehow also thrives as a problem-solving politician. And weaving through it all is a keen storyteller chronicling his well-seasoned observations with what he calls "non-fiction story poems."

Listen to him paying big attention with dirt under his fingernails:

> "The clockwork of seasonality can slip now, easy as a
> fan belt sliding on a pulley, stuttering before getting
> back on track..."

Well into a rich bold life of uncommonly diverse explorations, Josh wonders aloud what to glean from experiences when the contexts vary so wildly. The question comes from a life well lived. The answers (which are not answers) he works through, does the math, in accessible poetic and prose-poetic form right in front of us. Then he hands it to us infused with joy and warts and humor — as if it were a gift (which it is). If Only we can find the savvy within.

James Botsford
Publisher
Sandyhouse Press

Foreword

BY ROGER DUNSMORE

*M**any of you readers know that Josh Slotnick, with his wife Kim,* has been central to the organic farming movement in Missoula and Western Montana for nearly thirty years. You were accustomed to his friendly, energetic presence in their vegetable stand at the east end of the Saturday Missoula Farmer's Market, selling their beautiful, healthful produce for decades. Some of you have been in their farm fields or barn, seeing them weeding the rows of kale or onions, or helped harvest the small mountain of orange pumpkins, tossing them one person to another, in October. Or attended his Organic Farming Classes at the University in the Environmental Studies Program. Amidst all this blood, sweat, and tears, all this fertile happiness and earthly bounty, Josh has also found his voice as a poet.

This poetry is celebratory. It celebrates the searing heat and rainy, snowy cold, the dry or muddy earth's fecundity, the friendly gossip while weeding together, the fussy tractors and broke down irrigation pumps, the tall deer fences, a beloved farm dog, "sleek as the wind, smiling," the mosquitos, squeals of pigs, the planting of the orchard, the careful preparation of these greens and carrots and turnips for customer pickup, even the mashed end of a finger in a hasty truck door slam, as he describes the others waiting with him in the ER, or the easy banter of his two daughters preparing a meal for the field hands. In more recent years, serving as an elected county commissioner, he takes us inside meetings wherein we are privy to the tortured emptiness of bureaucratic language, or a dying mayor's gentle, empathic response to an over-the-top petitioner. Or honors his wife's careful skill for laying winter squash exactly for transport. Even celebrates white knuckle winter driving over Chief Joseph Pass, or a brief encounter with a hitchhiker on a cold morning, late for work on the reservation. These poems celebrate a life well-lived in the real mountain West — the grit, the conflicts, the grueling work, the camaraderie, the seasons in all their glory and hardship, the beauty and joy and pain of organic farming in the river bottoms of our lucky place in time and space.

And, Josh asks the questions any farmer-citizen, poet, or person of conscience and consciousness must ask these days, perhaps in any days, particularly in a community as attractive and conscious as Missoula, and especially for those elected officials who have the honor and responsibility for guiding and managing a growing, vibrant place —

" . . . can we make things better without destroying whatever real there once was, without sending already out of control rents into the stratosphere . . . ? Must beautiful, funky, interesting, historic, devolve into exclusive? Does reclaiming always equal gentrification? Must everywhere eventually become Ballard, Williamsburg, or a string of precious blocks on Magazine Street in the Garden District?

Can a place save its skin without selling its soul?"

The overall issue of how to respond to the growing numbers of homeless people among us, and Missoula's ability to come up with a creative encampment on the south edge of town, for which Josh was one of the primary political player's, is a small gesture in the face of these necessary questions. And the ongoing righteous work to make the best food locally available and to keep the ground itself, the waters and soils, healthy for the long haul is the backbone of his work as commissioner, to serve his community in its best practice of development, while also continuing to work as an organic farmer. And to teach, in the fields and in the classroom, in the meeting rooms, not only the youth but also the broader community, a way for a decent, respectful and long-term practical way of being here, in this body, on this incredible earth/home, among not only our fellow humans, but among all the forms of life with whom we share this now beleaguered planet.

And he asks those other, necessary, questions as well, when, after a "once a year, all day rain" lasts for two weeks and mosquitoes "swarm . . . thick as brambles" and "one day your knee begins to come apart . . . and now your leg just kinda works," he ponders, "Can all this be a part, none better or worse?/ Everything/ on its way to something else." In these poems, these questions, Josh Slotnick reveals himself as a true humanist of the soil, of his family and of the community: a plant whisperer of this old Garden City which traditionally grew the fresh vegetables for the miners working the copper out of the Butte hills.

In his own introduction to this collection Josh has mentioned the import of stories and storytelling and refers to these poems as "a book of poems that are . . . each a small non-fiction story." I might add what the great Pueblo storyteller, Leslie Silko, has to say about the power of stories. She says that they are all that we have to ward off the "Witchery" that is always about trying to destroy the world. And the best stories are kept in the mind in the belly. That mind down there. Because they are, essentially, visceral, in our guts. Or not. As Josh tells us, these poems are not an attempt at literature. They are the story of his farmer, soil-gut soul. Take the third one in. "Wish I could." It's a story about spreading manure out onto the fields, manure for the dirt which will cradle the seed until the moisture comes and the sun-warmth, and the seedlings push up through the dirt to bear fruit which we harvest and store and eat — eat plants that eat manure, eat light, eat water of late snows, ditch irrigation from the snow-melt rivers. Without the manure the soil will be mined out, nutrients extracted. Some say a bushel of Kansas wheat has sixty percent less protein than it did fifty years ago. And so farmers for centuries are out there spreading manure on the seed beds before the rains come to make it too muddy for the tractor, the spreader, and the disc. (Josh told me in a recent conversation that the world "manure" means, literally to work with the hands, has the word "hand" in it: *manus, hand,* from Latin.) In this poem he has to turn down an old, dying farmer who speaks and walks with difficulty, but is asking for his help in moving a piece of farm equipment with his front-end loader. And Josh has to turn him down, trying to beat the rain before it turns his field to mud.

> *I tell him about beating the rain, on another day*
> *no problem,*
> *but I have to see this through*
> *now*
> *Wish I could but I can't*

The old farmer, instead of anger, disappointment, or blame answers him with his own manure spreader story:

> *I used to load one of those by hand....*
> *One time I loaded the fucker up*
> *and the gear box broke off the wheel*
> *The cart hit the dirt*
> *I was shoveling it out, not close to empty*
> *my dad waves me off*
> *crawls under there on his back*
> *and pushes it up*

pushes the fucker up!
Goose eggs popping on his arms
I shoved a hunk of timber under there
He slides out and I told him. . . .
Dad
don't do that again

And the old man goes on then about the cancer in his lungs, in his kidneys, gives the finger to all that, the doctors wanting to cut on him once again:

I ain't goin' back there
that was '07
Indian friend of mine up on the highline sends me medicine
My weight goes up and down
But I'm above ground. . . .

I'm 78 fucking years old
Good luck, you beat the rain, I been there

I thanked him
and roared the tractor back to life
back to my life, to this one small job
in a rich, rich world
on an about-to-rain
fall day

This exchange between an elder and younger farmer amidst the pressures of weather, soil, and breaking-down machinery catches hold of that snatch of the "real voice" that is so often floating about us. Josh's capacity to catch it on the fly, so to speak, is itself a form of language-farming. Look/listen for it — in this little treasure of a book, and as you move about in your own world, office space or computer screen.

I like to think of Josh as our very own "Jew Boy" out of North Dakota (and by way of his Peace Corps years in Thailand): our homegrown, unofficial, organically savvy, farmer-poet-Rabbi, bringing the best of our oldest traditions into the life of this here/now/ongoing place. I hope I live long enough to see him in even greater positions of public trust. Reading his poems, I say to myself, *I like this guy. I'm glad he's a county commissioner. I'm glad he's a friend.*

PS. I have the habit of reading the last poem or short section of a book first, instead of starting at the beginning, in order to see if the book is going to take me to a place I want to go. So . . . if you have only the energy or inclination to read one poem today, and you want it to come from and go into that visceral mind deep down in the belly, read the last poem in this book — "To Danny Baum."

PPS. Reading Josh Slotnick's words, I am reminded of the Japanese poet Ryokan's statement:

> Who says my poems are poems?
> My poems are not poems.
> When you understand that my poems are not poems
> then we can begin to speak of poetry.

ROGER DUNSMORE taught Humanities and Wilderness Studies at the University of Montana from 1963–2013. He has published five volumes of poetry and a book of essays, Earth's Mind: Essays in Native Literature. His New and Selected Poems, On The Chinese Wall, 2018, is available from Drumlummon Institute.

Intro: Thanks For Picking It Up

*T*his *book stems from a life of farming, this season will be my 30th*. A farmer friend wondered out loud to me the other day about the finite amount of tries she had with tomato starts. She'd been at it 20 years, that only means 20 tries to learn from, with some finite amount left to go. What can we rightfully expect of ourselves in terms of learning from experience, when the context for that experience rides the vicissitudes of weather, culture, biology, and everything else, and any number of seasonal tries can't really be that many? I write this in spring, and this year a new and specific puzzle challenges us, alongside the old ones. How to keep this work in our lives to the right degree, and make space for someone else, and something else, an exit strategy of sorts. How many tries do we get at that? In this moment if I were to let myself mentally go to the farming demands of the immediate, I'd upend this table and sprint home, even as it is early in the morning on a Sunday. So much needs to be done. For decades just this, the immediate, family, land, plants, students etc. ate nearly every bit of brain space. The intensity of that life required absolute presence, so planning beyond the needs of the next season didn't make the to-do list, and the finitude of "tries" at anything didn't dent consciousness. Right now though, on the precipice of this 30th season, it's all there — the now, the future and the already gone. That's in these poems, an informed but shaky, awareness of time.

That awareness, the finitude of tries at all things, colors these poems, as does some wholly new experience — time spent in local civic affairs as an elected official. I love where I live, I am of this place, and a few years ago a natural impulse towards service, the right public need and a fully felt desire for a 3rd act, led me to run for office and radically change the life I had been living outside of our farm. I had about a year to learn this work in what now feels like a warm honeymoon in an older simpler world, the Before Times. Then the pandemic crashed in and changed every moment of how we did local government. Functionally, my job entails a ton of talking with people. I'm a County Commissioner and Missoula County is a big organization for Montana, we have nearly 1000 employees and we work closely with City, the non-profit community, trade associations, the private sector, community groups, other electeds and plenty of concerned individuals. This work demands deep focus, active listening, an awareness of history and context, recognition of physical cues and an understanding of the specific web of relationships that overlay any local collection of humanity. The pandemic sent us to our screens and all that kind of went to shit. We adapted as best we could, but as you know, talking with a 3-inch image is a thin facsimile of actually interacting with a person, and there's no substitute for the energy a group of people can create. The screens profoundly compromise anyone's ability to focus, perceive and ultimately understand, and yet we got by, kept the wheels on the proverbial bus while steering through a storm, and even made modest steps forward. Though we work in person now, things do not feel at all like they did before.

Uncertainty, another theme in these poems, has not just ramped up, buts seems to define this specific time in history. Not calling out the strands of this destabilizing force undervalues their intensity, so here goes: a wave of hateful anger followed a summer of racial reckoning and has crept into public policy, mid-century warring fascism in Europe is back, housing has become financially out of reach for people who live here (and nearly everywhere else), and climate disasters play ominous background music to all of modern life. This summer our valley could fill with smoke once again. That's a lot of uncertainty. This moment has infected so many of us not just with a potentially fatal respiratory virus, but a wits-end brittleness and a fatalistic failure of empathy.

During the pandemic, and maybe because of it, the golden age of storytelling amped up: prestige TV, podcasts, long-form journalism, novels and films — we seemed to have gotten even better at storytelling, and in ever new ways, and we've been telling each other stories for as long as we've had language. Stories elegantly allow us to inhabit the perspective of another. Think of a series, or a novel you got attached to in the past couple years — we empathize with admittedly, if not profoundly, flawed characters. We hope for them because the camera, or the words, allow us to see the world from their perspective. We quickly lose objectivity and emotionally join their side. We root for them. These flawed heroes fail in all the ways people fail, and we watch helplessly from the sidelines and eagerly click to the next episode, or turn the page, just to keep rooting for them some more, and to see what happens next. We link ourselves to their fate and put a small slice of our hearts on the line. Our current historical moment has caused me to wonder, is this level of empathy for those unlike ourselves possible when the stakes are greater than our viewing/reading/listening pleasure, when we are more than spectators to the drama?

Because of their low-risk, easy availability, stories seem to stretch us in ways real life just can't. I say all that because this rant is an intro to a book of poems that are essentially each a small non-fiction story. Could non-fiction story poems make little micro-bridges between our easy-crush empathy for flawed fictional characters and our national disease of disregard for real humans who think differently than we do? Is it the stakes, is that the dividing line between who gets empathy and who doesn't, real life vs. Netflix? If only we knew our neighbors as mere actors in a drama, then we might root for them too, but their reality seems to demand we write them off as evil or naïve if they don't see the world as we do. Well, if you wade through this intro, a thin chunk of non-fiction poetry is coming up next. Characters step into some of these poems, they are real people and I hope you root for them all, and possibly extend that grace to your actual neighbors. Please though, make no mistake, all this comes to you from a deeply limited and sharply specific perspective — if there's Truth here, you're finding it more than I'm chronicling it. Hopefully this intro sheds some light on that perspective.

My friend Danny Baum wrote about what he called "Third Act Trouble", the struggle to break the malaise that befalls some of us deeper into life, when, "if you haven't been displaced, you've dropped off the learning curve". What if you are wired for more yet, and even as you intentionally place yourself in challenging situations — an embrace of the new, you have a keen awareness of the temporariness of it all; how does that change your deliberations, responses, and relationships? The new will be old, soon enough. That awareness doesn't require a whole lot of perceptive skill. "Keen," here more means reality powerfully felt, than skills finely honed. Look around and every view is a wake-up-call to both the world's irrepressible will to change and our own personal irrelevance, from the dynamic pattern of spring snow melt in the hills, to the ontological dislocation of "adult children", to right-before-your-eyes gentrification. So, with all that weighty enough to knock me down if I dare stop moving, I've been tempting fate and pausing for an hour or so a week, to write poems in this vein. This writing isn't just an attempt to personally work on the koan of existence though, these poems re-tell events, line out stories, that if rendered skillfully, could be resonant enough to spin up some empathy. In this way these poems reflect more of an attempt at discernment than a try for literature. These poems document an ongoing effort to recognize good stories when they come by — we don't invent these types of stories, so much as we spot them when they enter our lives. This little volume is a collection of that effort from the last handful of years, written while wrestling with Third Act Trouble and a long-time farmer's round awareness of time, all in an age of profound and perilous uncertainty.

You may be deep into crafting your first or second act. Well, if you're as lucky as me, someday you will get to author a third, and maybe these words will land for you, or if you've lived through most of it already, these poem-stories could make you smile, cringe, or feel a catch in your in throat. One can only hope. Thanks for picking it up.

HOME

All of It Could Turn Out Just Right

A new young farmer called the other day looking for a pump
5 horse, 3 phase
did I know of one?

Years ago
at the turn of the millennium
on a blue bird fall day
I walked this place with Marvin Gallagher
while my young family
waited across town

We passed listing corrals, walked through a
slotted-with-daylight barn
around
a sway-backed abandoned milk house
gazed at his soaring new RV garage
with gleaming metal roof
and he told me what I needed to know
about the underground lawn irrigation
the clean-out for the septic
the well for the house

I told him how my wife and I would pull those corrals
till up the pasture
build a greenhouse, a wash shed, chicken coop
eight-foot fence — we were going to move our farm here

That spring, to dodge the bindweed seeds from the ditch
we also put in an irrigation well
Marvin's 5 horse 3 phase pump
that we never used
has sat, perched over the ditch, at the ready
ever since

I might have a pump for you
I said to the young farmer
I'll call you after I pull it

A corrugated metal cover wraps the
pump like a baby quonset roof
arched
just right
and slid into grooves
notched
into a platform of treated 2 x 6s
I needed a cheater bar to break the 4" union
Marvin teflon taped every junction
double hose clamped 2" poly over metal barbed fittings
grease still oozed from the zerks
He did every step
just right

I am fifty years old now
Our kids have moved on, those things I built when we first
came here
have weathered
I am 2/3 to where Marvin was, that shining fall day
at the turn of the millennium
when he stopped short my fast-paced list
of what I would do
to his place
our place, right then

He cut me off
with the gentle, hard hand of a schoolteacher

4

. . . . . . .Yeah
He said
I moved here in '61
in my early 30's, I had a couple little kids, a new business
was all full of piss and vinegar

He tapped a fat finger on my chest, sucked in a long
emphysemic breath

Just
like
you

———

Come pick it up
I said to the young farmer

Wish me luck
He said
Sure, but that's not it
Do what you know you ought to
every step
and all of it could turn out
just right

As We Should

FOR JUPE

She knew the kids' names
"other side of the truck", "wait here", "get that deer out"
She'd keep up with me on the tractor
driving
to the field around the corner
pinning her ears back, throwing those front legs out
she'd go horizontal in the air
pounding paws at speed along the ditch roadside
sleek as the wind, and smiling

Now I ratchet back the rpms on the way over
so she doesn't fall too far behind
Yesterday driving to the field around the corner
as we have always done
I caught the eye of a dude
zipping past
kayaks strapped to his Subaru
headed to the end of the road river access
He nodded
lifted the corner of his smile a bit, like he knew
I tried to imagine what he saw

An old timer farmer in a frayed ball cap on a tractor
a white-faced border collie
loping along side

Have we become a cliché
shallow, easy to read
like an image of
a sunset on the beach, a homeless guy pushing a shopping cart

or
a cool shades dude with kayaks strapped to his Subaru?

While I wonder at these things
our story becomes richer, even as our purchase on this life
grows thinner
Regardless
she knows better than to throw mental energy
in such a direction
At the field gate
she smiles up at me when I lift the fence chain
in awe of our great good fortune, to be here, now
with each other
once more
doing as we should

Wish I Could

Early October
spreading manure to beat the rain, to plant garlic
I rarely have this stress in fall —
soil too wet to till
that's a spring stress
But here we are, ground barely dry enough
the grey sky darkening
again the tops of the mountains
disappearing
into incoming fat foamy clouds

Astride a roaring tractor
I slam the front-end loader
the bucket
into a wind row of aged manure compost, and lift
a mountain of fertility for the coming season
The rest of this operation lays out in my head step by step
it will happen just so
and pretty quick
I'll fill the spreader, hook up the tractor, and this manure
will fly
then fall, in a dusty skein across the soon-to-be garlic beds
I'll unhook the spreader
put the spader on
and till it all in
The beds will be made by lunch
then let the rain come again
No matter

From the farthest right of peripheral vision
a man shuffles toward me

soiled jeans faded striped collared shirt
sleeves rolled above the elbow
He moves without rush, but
he wants something

Behind him a 90's truck and trailer outfit waits

Tractor side now, he starts to speak, then holds his breath
I pull the rpms down to idle
tractor noise you can talk over
but no words come
His round red cheeks flex up and down a few times
pursed lips bounce together
waiting, for words
for breath
then
a torrent

I only got one-and-a-half fucking lungs

I saw you and had to stop
You gonna be here all day?
I got a disc up the road, need to get it in my trailer, you could do it
with your loader
I got 160 acres in Grass Valley

Good for you, I said

Yeah I don't know about that

I tell him about beating the rain, on another day, no problem
but I have to see this through
now
Wish I could but I can't

I used to load one of these by hand, he points at
the manure spreader
we pulled it with horses
One time I loaded the fucker up and the gear box broke off the wheel
The cart hit the dirt
I was shoveling it out, not close to empty
my dad waves me off, crawls under there on his back and pushes it up
pushes the fucker up!
Goose eggs popping on his arms
I shoved a hunk of timber under there
He slides out and I told him
I says
Dad
don't do that again

I'm 78 years old
They took half my lung, fuckers
I got out and they say, the cancer's in your kidneys
they gotta go too

He held both middle fingers up high to the mountains
to the universe

Fuck that
I ain't goin' back there
That was '07
Indian friend of my mine up on the highline sends me medicine
My weight goes up goes down
But I'm above ground

Eyes wide, shoulders dropped, palms turned to the sky
he said
I'm 78 fucking years old
Good luck, you beat the rain, I been there

I thanked him
and roared the tractor back to life
back to my life, to this one small job, in a rich, rich world
on an about-to-rain
fall day

A Better World

I've been here since 6:45 in the morning
Setting up, taking money, restocking, chatting and standing
Now noon
the final half-an-hour of this market, and a dead lull settles in
like a wet cloud
Home, lunch, solitude call to every cell of me
but I am stuck here for 30 more minutes

A fit and famous international documentary filmmaker
bursts up to our stand
cracking the lull with raw energy
I'm so glad I made it, she says, breathing like a speed walker
it was such a push to get here
her yoga mat slung over one shoulder
like an arrow quiver
ath-leisure capris highlight bronzed and toned calves

I ask her about her latest trip, heard she was in Asia
for the Discovery Channel
Africa too
and toss in a mention
of my own modest winter adventures
to inspire conversation
build affinity
and convince myself
I am not a mere provider for people beyond me in station
impact and beauty
Maybe we really do share something
outside of this

She smiles, looks up from her basket — maroon tomatoes
saber-toothed anaheims
gaudy, super-model rainbow chard
and leans into her story:
Pandas
the new popular demand in China for a national park system
cutting edge ecological restoration in Kenya
She sets down her basket
Pushing her energy towards a crescendo
Her bluebird blue-sky eyes flash, her red hair, rich
as the sound of a cello
catches
the mid-day sun
her sharp hands cut the air, driving it all home

The world is getting better

She pays for $9 of food with a $100 bill
and scurries off
I smile
to have sold out of chard
almost all the tomatoes and peppers
and now
to go home

Complicit

It's me, after all who drives the car at 4:37 in the morning
Ice crunches in the gravel driveway
Ground blizzards sweep winding lines of snow
like snakes
racing across our empty county road

Who can speak at this hour, in this cold?
Even the usually swarming intersection a mile away is nothing
bare to the horizons
The nice people from the BBC chat on the radio, ignorant
of all this
Meanwhile, minutes from now we'll curve into
the airport turn-around
and you'll dissapear
Of course
this is how it's supposed to go
we should be used to it

How is it that I want to hold you like a lifeboat, and also
helped set you up
to leave
only to occasionally pop in like this and then disappear again
in a four-in-the-morning dream

Trying to Turn the Irrigation Pump
on to Prevent Frost Damage at 4:30
in the Morning in Early October

The irrigation ditch reflects thin wisps of silver clouds
and a rippling
upside-down moon
That fat full moon screams blue light down on this scene, bright
as highbeams
I lift up and push down the priming arm on the pump
Up and down up and down up and down
watch
my silhouette in moonshadow expand and retract, again and
again and again
but no water comes
I am too late
This hard cold has frozen
the water in the straw-like pipe to the ditch
The pump won't prime
I paint it with flame from a propane torch
but that's just to exhaust options
I know it won't work
doesn't work

The feathery silver clouds in running ditch water
the blaring billions
of four-in-the-morning stars
the grand moonlight in a frozen periwinkle field
don't care

I lost his one and am fine
just fine

Everything

Irrigation gaskets dry out, split, leak
Exhaust pipes rust
Paint chips
Bearings break free, every joint, no matter the grease
turns to gravel
Even your magic phone will go
belly up

One day your knee begins to come apart
Cords held for years start to fray, wear thin, like rope pulled
tight in the long day sun
day after day
Of course it went
Now your leg just kinda works
Like Andy the dentist said last month
That tooth is going south on you

This spring we had a once-a-year, all day rain
for two weeks
The heavy grey sky got stuck in our valley
like air trapped in a balloon
The hills greened up early, then got greener, and greener still
Now mosquitos swarm in the evenings
thick as brambles
Old snow still stripes the mountain tops
and heavy purple storm clouds
slow roll

in a dreamy pastel oil painting of a sky
at sundown

Can this all be of a part, none better or worse?
Everything
on its way to something else

Why I Did All That

Old enough
to have a few dead people
in my phone

Old enough
to desire only to be desired
and to know
what's left is melting like ice on the sidewalk
while the riches of a past world
fade like taillights
racing to the horizon

Moving irrigation pipe through rumpled waves of rising heat
the world baking in scorching August yellow
or making one more pass with the tractor, before the last light
of a late spring day
goes flat
I know this like I know my name:

All that came from me
is for you

Smoke Broken; a Millennium Epic

FOR THE LOST FALLS OF 2012, 2015, 2017

Fall

The sweet o' the year, the redemption of our labor
arrives every season
on schedule
From mid-September to mid-October
fall's cobalt sky spreads out and up, deep as any ocean
Sharp morning air demands a sweatshirt
afternoons warm to shirtsleeves
We pile, stack, box, bag and bin
medicine ball pumpkins
mountains of bright winter squash, carrots, beets, potatoes
onions onions and more onions
Mountains cut our skyline in crisp, knife-line silhouette
Fall comes like this
Always

Farm Family

We swam in this water, breathed in this air:
moving pipe, making snacks, changing diapers, loading trucks
napping kids in greenhouses, reading bedtime stories
hauling them and their gear — strollers, car seats
frontpacks and backpacks
to market
Working the flow of
crops to weed water harvest deliver
and infinity loops of laundry
All of this ran together like a braided stream

Certain as the seasons, forever as the sky
This became our way
I could imagine
no other

2000
First summer
of the new century
At 7, 4 and 1 our kids put us in the thick of it
We lived in accordance with the needs of our family
and what the seasons called for
These rock-solid guideposts set up certainty
an order to the world
beyond the questioning of words

A couple-hundred Hell's Angels roared through town
that summer
on their summer run, to a mountain retreat nearby
but downtown
just as many rent-a-cops in riot gear pushed through thick
throngs
of college students, townie kids, and wanna-be journalists
all sweating out a steamy night
hoping to catch a glimpse
of outlaw bikers
but the Angels stayed in camp, never even came downtown
The crowds on the street
swirled around clutches of Rainbow people
Yes, the Rainbow people were here too
In hemp shorts and dirty dreads
They milled about on corners, under awnings, by the river
waiting
to gather
with a thousand like-minded others in a national forest nearby

Late spring never came that year, we jumped right to summer
A line of 90-degree days in June
merged into weeks of triple digits by July
The sky turned chalky yellow with heat ripples, dust
and a relentless sun

The second night of the bikers
A lit interstate cigarette tossed from a 65 mile-an-hour
car window
set ablaze
a swath of knee high crunchy brown grass on Waterworks Hill

Decades ago, locals spray painted
a peace sign on a mega billboard-like structure
On the Hill
supposedly it had something to do with radar
to communicate
The peace sign stood over downtown, like a lighthouse
for generations

Now flames threatened to torch Peace, on stage
500 feet above downtown
Where, amidst the townie gawkers, rainbow people
and rent-a-cops
a drunken college kid fell off a tailgate cruising the main drag
hit her head hard
The rent-a-cops started in
tossing the crowd aside to get to the fallen girl
All that energy, ready to go, like the brown grass
and dead dry forest
just waiting, to explode
In the scrum, someone said something
incendiary
and it all went up in flames:
baton-cracked heads, zip tie handcuffs
clouds

of pepper spray and screaming sirens
Kid rent-a-cops
dragged college kids
to jail

The Bitterroot mountains to the south caught fire
Towering flames poured grey billowing smoke clouds
into our valley, like steam from a kettle eternally forgotten
A slew of sooty sky 100-degree days
merged into weeks
Streetlights came on mid-afternoon

It was, after all, Y2K

———

The New Century
'03 and '07 came
without the visiting characters
but burning nonetheless
The gunmetal sky with a campfire stench returned
cut short
the farming season
and grabbed your throat
with an angry hand
2012's smoke devoured fall
ate the entire season, the sky, the mountains
made runny-nose flatlanders of us
obliterating
our rolling craggy horizon
The heavy smoke spread cough, snot, and melancholy
like pollen on the wind
2014 brought more of the same and now
again

———

Now

I am on my knees in the potatoes
Ash falling like snow
and I know
2000 did not bring a one-time millennial curse
The roar of the Harleys
wheezed a death rattle big as the universe
not for the century
but for
the seasons

The clockwork of seasonality can slip now, easy as a fan belt
sliding on a pulley
stuttering before getting back on track
In these breakdowns
Fall can get lost, like keys or sunglasses, until maybe it returns
Right now Sophie — she was 4 in 2000, is packing
to leave

How do we live in accordance
with
a discordant universe?

Are we obligated to call it out
when the best might be happening in front of us, now
and not wait for memory?
I should I have said it out loud, named that time, so long ago
slowed down long enough to really drink it in
when the kids were small, golden
holding to us
and the beauty of fall
shined
for always

Bananagrams at Christmas

How can I
absorb you all, all at once
and

PEEL!

This room, full as my heart, and how
to place a "Y" with no "L"
in my temporary arrangement
while your voices color everything, I want to listen
to every word
I don't care about the words

PEEL!

My stack of letter tiles grows
Can't I just cook for you, drink you in?

PEEL!

I need to undo what I have made
all to find
a place for an "X" and an "F"
Two steps back, hoping to take one forward
We won't have you back again till
July
But now, all is right with the world
I don't want anything
to undo that

PEEL!

Fearless at 11, Sandlot Football and Our 70's divorce

SYRACUSE, NY, CIRCA 1976

2 on 2, and 2 completes is a first
4 Mississippi rush
We played in an empty lot
in an old-school city neighborhood
clapboard houses with narrow potholed streets
frost–heaved sidewalks
soaring roadside trees

One kid goes out for a pass, a kid covers him
another rushes the quarterback
1 Mississippi, 2 Mississippi, 3 Mississippi, 4 Mississippi
My friend Greg quarterbacks, sprinting to the sideline trees
head up, elbow cocked
he twists from outstretched arms
our buddy's hands
grasping
for a shoulder, shirttail, ankle, anything

Greg would be Fran Tarkenton, I'd be John Gilliam
like we saw on Monday Night Football
I can still hear the opening music
My parents, distracted from fighting, didn't make me go to bed

They were parents to us, all we knew
Our mother, afraid to drive, braided my little sister's hair
hugged us tight enough
to break a rib
Introduced Cat Stevens, Carol King, Carly Simon
dancing in the living room

and unpredictable explosions
Our dad couldn't crack the code
of her episodic tears
or the cryptic words of his coworkers
But he'd exclaim, Hey Bud, see that license plate
3 primes in ascending order!
He puzzled strangers
but not me
I translated for visiting friends, the grocery clerk
the Carvel ice cream girl
He painted a technicolor animal mural
for my sister
and stuck with me tight at 9
through every shaking-scared moment
of a first-year hitless little league season

My sister and I couldn't see the coming tsunami
of our 70's divorce
upheaval to a distant houses-all-look-the-same Beltway suburb
and mega-middle school
where kids watched all the TV they wanted
in their bedrooms

I launch for the ball, fully extended, horizontal, hands tilted up
open
fearless at 11
The patchy-grass, hard-scrabble earth, here in the middle of the lot
will not forgive
My friend's big brother sprinting behind me launches too
And he's got me
by 2 years and 20 pounds of thick knees and sharp elbows
ready to pin my scrawniness
to the dirt
But I am long, sinewy, flying
and I've got him
by a step

Tarkenton threw sidearm, falling off the sideline
a Chicago Bear
clawing into his back
Gilliam, stretching to impossible proportions
mocking gravity
would make the catch

I see the ball in slo-mo
the laces, the stripes, spinning down
to my open hands
I believe
in the permanence of this time
I believe
I can catch anything

Notes to Self

FOR YOU AND IKKYU

Feel the skin on her side, just below the ribs
the softness
a golden silken glow
the smell
the heat rising
her sounds in your ears
All this has a shelf life, a window

Soon the churning engine of memory
relentless as the calendar
will spin all this beauty into narrative, will make sense of it
in words
and this glowing moment will become
something else

Make yourself stop
feel all of it
let it be in you straight, no chaser
like breath

Because too quickly
this too will become just, story

The silver sky, faded-snow mountains, slick-shimmery pavement
smell of you on my hands
We make the world with our senses
then spin sensation into
stories

But the world carries on just fine without us
story-less
impassive, even to itself

Feel that

Hey Little Man

FOR OSCAR, BECAUSE NOW WE KNOW

I don't know your name yet
but when I saw a kid close to your age the other day — a baby
and because
that's what you will be in just a few weeks
I missed you
like I miss your dad, and I saw him yesterday
He shines like the platinum mountain tops in spring
on the edge of the town of your birth
his birth
People pull to him like gravity
They know better than to question what they feel with words
you will see it your whole life
Or your aunts — I can barely type that without welling up
I miss them so much
Their steadfast love for you makes the shapes of these mountains
seem transitory
and they cut the same lines against the grey sky
as they did
in grainy 19th century photos
when tipi rings clustered along the river flats

Welcome back

LOCAL
GOVERNMENT

Thread the Needle

Josh Slotnick
Sent: Mon 2/15/2021 10:47 AM
To: Juanita Vero, David Strohmaier
Cc: Chris Lounsbury

Subject: RE: Post Office

As per Dave's earlier note, the smackdown council endured a few years back is apples to oranges with this current incarnation of moving the post office. That was before my time, so mine's more of a 30,000' view. Suffice to say, it shouldn't be a can of worms, given the new landscape there's no need to kick this can down the road any further, we should be able to move forward without letting the perfect be the enemy of the good. Dave, I'm glad you can run this issue to ground w the Mayor and Dale. We'll get it sorted. They do seem kind of augured in on this, hate to see them get wrapped around the axle before we've really begun, but when their knickers are in a knot it can be tough to talk 'em off the ledge. If anyone can do it though, Dave you can. These guys are on our team, we've got to go all carrot here, no stick. I'm glad you're on it, I'd just get out over my skis real quick and throw fuel on that fire. Before we know it, the wheels'd be off the bus and we're eddy'd out on this thing for months. That's a perfect storm we could actually avoid. I get that this proposal isn't fully baked yet, but sometimes you just have to build the airplane while you're flying it. I know you guys kicked tires on this one before my time, and Council could point fingers all day, but like an ex-governor once said, "that dog don't hunt". This Federal Building project is more than a new coat of paint on an old fence, and we didn't even have a dog in that Post Office fight a few years back. Best bet here is to bite the bullet and call out the elephant in the room, and yes, it's big, but we'll just have to eat it one bite at a time. Anything less would just be re-arranging the deck chairs on the Titanic, and at the end of the day, who has the bandwidth for that?

Gotta run, as usual my cart's ahead of its horse.

Josh Slotnick
Missoula County Commissioner
406 239 6993

A Pre-pandemic Story

Take my picture
her voice came at me garbled
but I could hear her smile
twin respirators muffling the tones
She held a cauliflower, dense, gleaming white, too big and heavy
to sell at full price
without jokes about mortgages and interest rates

Cauliflower in hand, my wife stood in a lush field of vegetables, our farm, on the west side of the Missoula valley.
Wildfire smoke bathed the scene in grey, ate the horizons,
obliterated the mountains and colored everything in sight.
At that very moment the last of Hurricane Harvey's bib-
lical rains pummeled Houston: 19 trillion gallons of water
fell in five days, more than four feet of rain, while Irma bore
down on the entire state of Florida, having already swept
away good chunks of Barbuda, Puerto Rico, and Cuba.
On the other side of the earth, new rivers coursed through
Mumbai, atop city streets. Surging urban torrents pulled fleeing people into open manholes and swept them out to sea.

Local Montana news provides updates on percentages
of fire containment, evacuation areas
event postponements
National media features colorful stories
gushes for the Cajun Navy
using bass boats
to save stranded neighbors, plucking pets off rooftops
while fetid water laps
at the cleaving eaves
of suburban homes
The people of Albany, Beaumont, Houston, Miami, New Orleans
Denton, Montana

are made of tougher stuff
and will put the pieces back together
We always do

Therein lies the heart of it

Bridges collapse and we have an infrastructure review, white
supremacists use cars as weapons and statues start to come
down, in the wake of this year's fires and storms and floods
we harvest cauliflower in the smoke
kayak through sewer water
do what needs to be done
and talk about
how strong we are

Scientists, struggling for defendable levels of accuracy
shy from certainty
We who work on the ground do not carry those obligations
can speak this straighter truth

Stories of resiliency
make it worse

Best Meeting Ever

We started the student farm on an old army fort
They interned Japanese and Italian people there in WWII
In the 70's the Psychology Department
repurposed the brig for experiments
on monkeys
We built a greenhouse next to the boarded-up shell of all that
moved into a corner
of a cavernous 19th century horse barn
tilled up a couple acres
and started in
Vegetables grew, students signed up, the grey ground went green

Two seasons later
big-time bird researchers, ornithologists, took our barn space
New walls, floors, windows, a 100-yard wind tunnel
Everything, 6 figures
state of the art
Their booming voice leader scored million-dollar
defense contracts
legions of graduate students
and reportedly
had a TV series already in the can

We moved the farm barn to an abandoned garage
on the other side of the old fort

The farm field lay between the shiny new avian research facility
and the Bitterroot River
where Native American students built sweat lodges
in a riverside slough

off the edge of a steep bank
in an ancient clutch of frayed cottonwoods and a thatch
of red willow
thick as the hair on a dog's back
You couldn't see those sweat lodges until you were
right on top of 'em

In the waning moments of the millennium
The University administration summoned us all
to a serious conference room
Indians, farmers
and scientists

Dr. Christian, Director of the Division of Biological Sciences
presided
His sharp silver hair topped a baby smooth narrow face
a Patagonia pullover gave bona-fides
to his rugged
outdoor field scientist status
but didn't hide
his yellow power tie and crisp white collared shirt
A group of Indians stood along the back wall
arms crossed
some in leather jackets, some in full regalia

At the table
a small balding rounded Environmental Studies professor
leaned in
two Native American student leaders nearby
didn't move
The penitent farmer
sat on his hands
An Executive Vice President for Special Projects
Special Assistant
to the President

in trimmed silver beard and deep navy-blue blazer
with state flag pin on the lapel
elegant like a 19th century soldier at court
sat to the right of Dr. Christian
The Environmental Studies professor, a union man with a long
eastern-European last name
scanned the room with fiery eyes
He twitched in his seat, itching with strategy
foaming for a fight

The farm needs to move, proclaimed Dr. Christian
Pale blue eyes
flashing like searchlights
*We require biological connectivity between the avian research facility
and the riparian area*

Cabbage, collards, long-haired grubby kids
something fouled the works
of experimental design, data collection, structural analysis
the farm must go, has to move
now
Chop Chop!

How about the sweat lodges?

Said a voice from against the wall
Leather jackets crinkled
the floor ached with the rustling
of shifting weight

Dr. Christian gripped the podium above the insignia
of our university
and in the last moments of the 20th century said
in a voice
chipper as an offer to come to breakfast

We will relocate the Native Americans

No one moved, no noise, nothing

We will relocate the Native Americans

A sharp abrasive scrape broke the silence
like tires
squealing at a traffic light

The Executive vice president for Very Special Important Things
had slid his chair back
hard enough to gouge the floor
He jumped to his feet
caught the back of the chair as it fell

I have to go, he spat downward into his crisp little beard
fleeing
like a man on fire

Dr. Christian continued, undaunted
*The presence of the sweat lodges compromises our ability
to achieve our research goals*

At the back of the table, a Native American student leader
cleared his throat
stood up
and spoke, as if calming a scared child

*No, no, you don't understand, Mr. Christian
we'll pray for your project too*

Time has lost who said what next, or how this exchange ended
but the professor passed the farmer
the following note

Best meeting ever!

Last Thoughts on Senate Bill 92

OFFICIAL COMMENT ON STATE SENATE BILL 92, A BILL THAT WOULD
MAKE THE COUNTY ELECTIONS ADMINISTRATOR AN ELECTED POSITION

(for maximum effect, read with Hamiltonian, fierce, breathless urgency)

I come before thee dignitary with humble commentary
My eyes cast down but my hearts spread round
cuz I'm here speakin' true
against SB92

Protection for the election!
Rejection
Of this
Hard-headed hard-hearted hard knocks power grabbin'
finger jabbin' rabid nabbin'
subliminal political criminal
frustration legislation

That's the dark toothy maw of this wanna be law

Appointed not anointed!
The administrator is greater, not a partisan artisan
but a skilled technician
So stop your fishin' for political wishin'
We're gonna hire the best for the job
protect integrity from the mob
This doesn't need to be so tense, lets save runnin' races
for when it makes sense

Do you get the time rhyme
Is it 1968 or 1865 I've
just got to ask
depends who's behind the Covid mask

Big tech protection from communication collection incites
more insurrection
cause nobody's got the tenacity for veracity
in this process mess
Don't throw fuel on that fire, desire
instead to put this to bed
Call this what it is
a technical position
There's no place for a mission
other than mathematical perfection of an air-tight election

Don't be a dog chasin' a car
Listen up
This is where we actually are:

Malefactors detractors reactors
bad actors
throwin' slop from every electronic roof top
Maybe your voice too
finding remedy in identity like Pence
Bankin' on bank
and
grievance
But you say oh well, it don't matter, so the big guy's
mad like a hatter, it's just game
and this before us today
is simply another play
If you had power you'd do the same

No
No need to add this to the mix, don't you remember January 6?
You all be messin' with fire — fiery, fired up, fired on
look at how far this has gone!
Hacks w open Glocks standin' guard over the voting box
wreaks
of partisan corruption

Eruption
of rage on rage, turn back the page and look around
you'll get this battle and the whole thing comes fallin' down
cuz its not built on rock or stone
but blood and bone
and belief
And when its gone
we're something other than we've been, even if your candidate's in

Ask yourself
Is that really what you want

Letter to the Editor

Lyndon Baines Johnson, the notoriously crass 36th president, fast-walked down a wide sidewalk in urban Dallas, flanked by aides and reporters moving from one important thing to the next. He abruptly stopped and the whole entourage did too. He laid a hand on a young aide's suitcoat shoulder, gently pulled him in close, and pointed across the street. A ragged man slumped against the wall of a building, head down, legs stuck out into the sidewalk. LBJ barked to the fresh-faced aide loud enough for everyone to hear, "You know what the difference is between that guy over there, and you and me?"

Holding his thumb and index finger an inch apart, he put his hand in front of the young aide's face and said, "about this fuckin' much!"

The pandemic came and
the homeless shelter cut to half capacity
People
became trespassers
feral, like post-apocalyptic refugees
hunkered
down by the river
Tarps fluttered in the cottonwood red willow floodplain
Garbage dumps grew
grocery carts died akimbo in the mud, up-ended
choc-a-bloc
Someone built a dugout of sticks and lumber wrap
All of this
along the banks of our beloved river

And so many saw it
while driving over the bridge to Best Buy

Amazing Dave's
or Target

Fires burned under the bridge
The Montana Department of Transportation feared
infrastructure catastrophe
And soon enough, spring's high water
will subsume
all of it

A blizzard of angry email clogged in-boxes, demanded
attention

Arrest them, buy 'em bus tickets to Spokane, get 'em out,
for God's sake
Clean It Up!

———

A private landowner offered some of their property
on higher ground
for a Temporary Safe Outdoor Space
a sanctioned camp
Service providers provide services
but This
is so much more than That
We needed to build a mini village
Meanwhile, meetings begat side conversations on services
and meetings
and capacity issues
for months
Then
Missoula County stepped in to manage the project
United Way took point on logistics
The Office of Emergency Management folks
worked closely with

everyone
The Board of County Commissioners secured CARES funding
Hope Rescue Mission took on day-to-day operations

They'll staff it 24/7
platforms and tents will replace shredded tarps
blowing in the wind
It'll be well-kept, orderly
Security will protect the people who live there
and nearby businesses
A bus stop
waits over by the Walmart
It will not be perfect, we will learn from our mistakes
Everything
might get better

Bear with us

AWAY

Winter Driving

We ignored the radio warnings
denied the flat grey sky, fat specks of snow beginning to spiral
just went for it
At 80 miles-an-hour we hummed down highway 90
smooth and weightless
a comfy couch flying through space in a bubble
of warmth and family
Music, podcast stories
SAT words quizzed
from a phonebook-thick volume of knowledge
The weather we desired
swirled
inside the car

We'd headed south
first the Pattagucci store in Dillon
long johns for all
Then north again, to Elkorn hot springs
where hot water
sputters from the earth, no matter the season
We caught the front end of the storm
before the plows
We
busted growing drifts up Grasshopper Canyon
skittered over ridged ice
and made the hot springs just fine

While soaking neck deep
in hot water
the big clouds cracked open
and snow-filled wind screamed in from every direction
All light left the sky
by 4:00

Post soak I grabbed thin coffee in the empty lodge
asked the kid for a reminder
How many miles to Jackson, for gas

No gas in Jackson
gotta make it to Wisdom
unless you get gas at the bar down the hill, $4.50 a gallon though

I did the ¼ tank calculus
Counting miles, we would make it
on the road
But stuck in the ditch all night
slid off the black-ice, rutted path highway
augured into a 6' snowbank wall
running the engine for heat 5 minutes every hour till dawn
maybe not

Two guys and the barkeep cluster at the bar
in an empty cavernous log building dance hall
Heard you had gas here?
Guy number 1 cranes his neck from the bar, vomits syllables
a burst of shitfaced slurred-word nonsense
Guy number 2 doesn't raise his head
The barkeep leaves his perch, walks around the bar
points
to a wide black window
See that light, in the side lot, that's the gas pump
A tiny beacon flickered in the blizzard
The snowfield parking lot, coated in 10" of fresh fluff
had no edges, no tracks, no clear path in
or out
The pump works, but the numbers are busted, you gotta multiply by three
leave cash or a card with me

I hit it hard
all acceleration and roar

got gas and followed our tracks back
into a white-out
down the open middle of the road
through the empty heart of the Big Hole valley
up up up
towards Chief Joseph pass
on one lane of half-ass skating rink road
where a gusting wind backhands our Subaru
and dizzying snow squalls spiral into the headlights

Alone it wouldn't matter
I have driven roads like this my whole life
but they sleep, all around me
A hot-water soak, sure and certain
warm car sleep
So I do
the little I know
for sure and certain:
Hold tight to the icy center
thread disaster
stay off the brakes, turn into a skid
don't overcorrect

The storm doesn't make it over the pass
but we do

At a better-than-you'd-think restaurant in Darby
they debate pizza toppings
I sip ice water, and listen
only because
I love the sound of their voices
My shaking knees
faintly rock the table

It'll Be Quick;
Crossing a Day in July, 2020

Taking big strides and little time — gotta move water
from one line to the other
race to the other field to help the crew
harvest 300 chard bunches for the Growers' co-op
and start cooking by 5:30
I see the steps to an intern cabin listing
slouching into the earth
and I've heard the complaints
A wooden stake and a couple screws, no problem
It'll be quick

I hold the steps up and out of the way with my left hand
and don't let go
With my right, I push a stake into the ground
just hard enough to keep it from falling
and raise up a single jack — a short-handled sledgehammer
A couple whacks and the stake will be set
I'll lower the steps, throw a few screws in and all will be
plumb, level and sturdy enough
for a few more months
It'll be quick
I'm already in the irrigation, driving to the field
around the corner
This is a one-handed move

As I'm lowering the blow with the sledge
the stake slips back, tilts
just enough
and at the perfect moment
so I undershoot it

The sledge drives the top of my finger down
the edge of the wooden stake
lifting back the skin and pulling it off
like peeling an apple

For a moment
you wait and wonder
Is this enough
to matter

At a pop-up tent in the parking lot of the ER
a masked and face-shielded older volunteer
thermometer-zapped my forehead
and directed me to take a seat
on the curb
arcing away from the building
six feet
from the next guy
I held a blotchy red rag on my hand
He clutched his elbow
Sleeveless flannel shirt, veiny ripped brown arms
60 year-old skin, ball cap
grey goatee sitting in a 9-day beard
Logging accident, he said
there's a piece of wood in there

The afternoon sun slid just low enough to clip the top
of the building
sending a crescent moon slice of shade
along the curb
but the concrete still held the heat of the day

A pregnant lady in a taut red and white striped tank top
paced behind her man
sitting on the curb
12' away

He stared at his feet, she caught my eye
This is so fucked! She said, pacing faster
Our doctor gets test results back and says
he's got to get to an ER
right away
and they won't even see him! No one knows what the hell is going on!

Six feet from them
a young dude with tiny dreads
stretched his legs out onto the parking lot pavement
one sandal-less foot wrapped in a white T-shirt
stained maroon
He looked west, towards the long -day July sun
like a man watching waves
from a pier

Rush hour rose to a steady roar on the four-lane road
beyond the parking lot

A silver Honda civic screamed towards our curb
stomp-on-the brakes stopped
The door opened half-way
unleashing
rhythmic screaming

Three nurses in haz mat suits and enough PPE for
a nuclear waste site
ran to the car and extracted a 400 lb. man
in a smooth motion choreographed to lift, shift and slide him
onto a wheelchair
They've done this before
The purple of one of his calves jumped out against
the white of his shorts
Its burning burning so bad fuck! Aaghh!! He screams
They disappeared into the hospital

You would've never known
the parked crooked silver Honda hadn't been there all day

The mountains to the east caught pre-sunset alpen-glow
throwing back yellowy orange glowing light
onto the peaceful
parking lot

I'm parched
you all want anything
The logger said
his voice buttery gravel
One arm cradling the other, he walked off
towards the convenience store on the corner

I made conversation with the couple — recent emigres
from Michigan
mountain biking, lost restaurant jobs, baby coming
he'd been feeling shitty for weeks — now this

In November, in this final slice of day, deer become silhouettes
the last of shooting light

A nurse stepped out of the building clutching a tablet, glowing
in the near dark
and barked
though her mask

Where's my elbow guy?

Letter from Santa Cruz,
Black Friday, 2018

Firestorms rock California
Nothing like this has ever happened, except last year
when 10,000 houses burned in Santa Rosa
Imagine that
This year they say even more structures have gone up
Grass fires roll over bony hillsides at 60 mph, trees crown
exploding into flames
like giant torches, shooting embers into the Santa Ana wind
These embers settle on rooftops miles away
Fire leapfrogs from house to house, neighborhood to
neighborhood
turning houses, cars, buildings
into smoke
The sprawling mega-city of San Jose chokes, schools close
people wear respirators, indoors

We've driven to California on middle-age, off-season farmer
vacation: 6 days of bike touring between the clean air coastline
and the inland vineyards of the Santa Yanez mountains, then
off to rendezvous with adult daughters at an AirBnB in Santa
Cruz for Thanksgiving. The younger one works in California,
the older one is in her last year of college in the east. She's
flown out to see her younger sister and us for the week. At
the end of all this the two of us will leave the car and head to
Mexico to see our son. My wife and daughters walk Santa Cruz'
downtown, on this, the day after Thanksgiving, the worst day/
best day of the year for consumer culture. I have gone to the
Santa Cruz Ultramat to wash our clothes, crusty and stinky
from 6 days of biking and camping. Don't let the name take
you in, there's not much ultra about the "Ultra"mat. I picked

it because the computer in my pocket said it was close, and
they had Wi-Fi and coffee & tea — I thought I could wash our
clothes and beat on this laptop while waiting out the afternoon.

Today the universe wryly smiles on scorched California
It's raining
raining sheets of rain
Surely the newly denuded hillsides will begin sliding
towards the ocean
taking out luxury homes and hairpin highway curves
That's what happened last year
But for now, the rain has brought all the shit in the sky
down to earth
Clean rain crispness has washed away
the acrid, catch-in-the-back-of-your throat bite
of smoldering plastic

Oldies music fills the Ultramat. I unload dirty clothes to
CCR, get quarters to Aretha, by the time I've bought tea its
Aerosmith. Inside the 1950's cut-the-corner-of-the-building en-
trance of the Ultramat, a skinny balding guy with a 9-day beard
lays back in a metal chair. He's the hypotenuse to the chair's
right angle. His head's dropped back and his mouth has fallen
fully open, like he's awaiting a dentist, but he's sawing logs.

A woman reeking of cigarettes with a face like topo map
approaches my little table
and asks
if I have a chip yet
So the government can watch you
She adds that she resisted as long as she could, but
they found her
I give her a *hmmm*, look her in the eye
and nod
She gives me a, "what can you do about it", shrug
and shuffles off

I put our clothes in a dryer, slip quarters into black slot obliv-
ion, and watch the machine spin before walking back to my
computer and tea by the window. Via text I learn the younger
daughter plans to leave a day early. We've made her crazy, as
only parents and siblings can. Now the older daughter's angry
at her. A short lifetime of playing certain roles seems to have
condemned us to the same behavioral songs over and over.
Our very own oldies station, and we know the songs really
well because we wrote 'em. The younger's daughter's put her
foot down. Fuck this, she's said. She's changing the station
and going back to her new life. Soon, it'll just be us again.

The sleeping man by the door has righted himself
He's standing tall
just a few feet from me, but turned away, nose to the window
facing the sheets of rain and singing to the music
He's not just singing to the Ultramat's radio though
he's swaying-singing
eyes closed, hugging himself, inhaling the song
belting it out

Let it rain
Let it rain
Let it rain
Rain
Rain
Rain

Signs of the Times;
December 12, 2021, Missoula, Montana

Gun metal grey December sky spits half-ass rain
A week of relentless small to-do fires
a few tragedies narrowly averted
intractable problems heavy and present as this sky
and now, 8:00 Sunday morning
a couple hours to do
as I wish:
type, strike, step back, stumble dance through poems
at a coffee shop
on a rainy Sunday morning

Feed chickens and then I'm gone

But wait, passenger side front tire of the old car rides low
almost too thin to drive on
I look at the puddles, the mud, my clean pants
and decide not to rig up the compressor and do this here and now
instead
I'll limp to a gas station and get air en route
to green tea and a toasted bagel with butter, a window
onto the rain, and this laptop

Next to a small red metal "Free Air" placard bolted
to a stained cinder block wall
a faded corporate ad poster of smiling summer fun people
on the lock-and-key metal cage
for barbeque propane tanks
shouts "$21.99"
An unpracticed hand has crossed that out in fat black sharpie
and scrawled, "$25.99"

The pale maroon air hose hangs from its wind-up roller
flaccid, jagged edged, and useless
Someone has cut the business end off
I turned away, and caught words, hand-placed, letter by letter
under the gas station's roadside declaration
of prices

"Give thanks for the little things"

Letter From New Orleans,
February 8, 2020

Sunday morning, 62°, schools-of-fish clouds swim up-
stream against a blue backdrop; the sky always on the way
to something else. Here, on the economically saner edge of
the Garden district, on Magazine Street, down a block of
buckled sidewalk, Caribbean colored houses nee' businesses, stand shoulder to shoulder with ultramodern glass and
steel neo-industrial apartments, caddy corner from clas-
sic NOLA homes — shotgun style run-on houses with tall
windows, painted shutters and skinny column porches.

Up the street
shiny metal framing pierces a scraped lot and pushes up
towards the sky
The old giving way to
apartments, condos with names, ground floor retail
Down the street
Work-site chain link guards a wrinkled patch of concrete
surrounds a crumbling building
Wild greenery tall as a person grows through the cracks
Giant flakes of stucco have fallen
from two stories up
revealing stacked bricks
faded red, some the color of marrow and some
stained near to black
The building's coming down, someday
Should have happened quite a while ago and when it's gone
well
like the sky
soon enough every neighborhood becomes
something else

Here, in early morning clarity, questions come rapid fire: can we make things better without destroying whatever real there once was, without sending already out of control rents into the stratosphere and further sorting people? Will beautiful, funky, interesting, historic, always devolve into exclusive? Does reclaiming have to mean gentrification? Must everywhere eventually become Ballard, Williamsburg, or a string of precious blocks on Magazine Street in the Garden district?

Can a place save its skin without selling its soul?

Like a kid dragging feet to get to school
NOLA fights back against this national disease
passively
A deep, deep rough around the edges pull toward the rumpled
wrinkled, hung over
we'll-get-to-it-later seems to have
slowed that shit right down
Local governmental participation in gentrification
does not appear to be as enthusiastic
or as drastic
as in other
more-naive places
Note the buckled sidewalks, pot-holed streets
crumbling buildings
waiting years for demolition
NOLA's seen it all and just doesn't get too worked up
This too will pass

If only

Some of What I Saw While Waiting at the Phoenix Airport for My Elderly Father to Drive Three Hours from Rural Arizona Because I Couldn't Pick up a Rental Car as My Driver's License Had Expired

A thin, smooth-skinned, shit-eatin'-grin, boy-faced man with
fashionable sun-glassed girlfriend striding alongside
Her arms swing, hips shimmy, runway proud
His moss-colored T-shirt says

I find your lack of ammo disturbing

A woman gesticulating to her friend at a coffee shop table
hands slicing the air
Her black eyes shine like wet olives, so black I want to look
again
I remember a white gauzy jumper, straight shiny hair
just as black
falling on café-au lait shoulders
but I don't look back, as her beauty
is not for me

A middle-aged man, shaved head, in a coal-colored tank top
with inked, sculpted
and impressive
grapefruit round, gym rat shoulders
His shirt says

Affliction

People clustering outside in a pocket park sculpture garden
as if to ward off the cold

but the weather is Arizona spring perfect
They commune in clutches of smoky love — oh delicious
cigarettes
talking through long draws
in Russian Chinese English, laughing
in billowy exhales
If only we all had such easy
small paths
to joy

A barista shuttles behind her bar
quick as a point guard
Her purple dread extensions bounce
Her eyelashes bend upwards like ski jumps
her nails
fabulous

She calls me hon, and
I feel better

One, and the Same

Only middle-aged men in the coffee shop early Sunday
grey haired heads bent
into newspapers
laptops
The men sit like planets in pattern
stuck
in slow moving orbit
Each one a specific private world

My right-hand slaps at the keyboard like a spastic toddler
Because
it is not whole
The index finger and ring finger must now work around
their wrecked neighbor
The Finger
Its been flipped, but always in jest
visited
wonderful places
gripped
with its mates
wrenches, pens, hoes, rakes, shovels, sockets, shoulders
Now though
it's pulled up, out of the action
but most definitely
in the way

Angry black stitches caterpillar crawl in a shaky line
from one side of the fingernail
around to the other
This very last part of an extended me pulses like
a lighthouse beacon
Blood thump thumping to a bulbous, yellow, maroon

numb and crushed
fingertip
with a nail split and blackened like a Cajun fish

Last Sunday, the last of the day, just this one last task
I don't want to do
Grimy sweaty greasy, lips chapped, stomach growly
water bottle long empty
late already for dinner
to a friend's I never see anymore
I race
in the new old truck
to the field around the corner

You, dear reader, me, we all know the dimensions
of our well-used machines
the way we know
the arc of our partner's shoulder blades, curve of their ribs
I didn't know this new old truck like that yet
just started using it

In one sweeping motion, a brushstroke of movement
I'm out the truck door
long-stepping
to the gate
already
in the job at hand
but that last piece of an extended me trails behind
and the thrown closed door
catches it
like the slamming jaws of a trap
I have to open the door
with my other hand
to free myself
to stare at the crushed and dented fingertip
waiting to decide, *does this matter?*

Then
the fingertip explodes, the top peels back
It's almost off
Blood
soaks through the sleeve cuff I death grip
sprays the stickshift guard Jackson Pollack style while whipping
through gears
on the drive to the hospital

When I ask
the younger-than-me ER doc if the weekend's been busy
He says
We mostly see injuries like yours
You're typical

An ER doctor friend from another time and place
once told me
There's grain to flesh and bone
and heart
We all break along the same lines
We're all mostly
the same

Here at this coffee shop, grey-headed solo worlds
each as one-of-a-kind
as the jagged line around my finger
with their own
one-of-a-kind backstory
sit apart
unique
but interchangeable
as we all are, most likely
broken
in the same kinds of ways

SKINNY OLIVE-SKINNED
JEW BOY ON THE HIGH PLAINS
GETS MISTAKEN FOR
MEXICAN, IRANIAN,
LIVES IN RURAL SOUTH-EAST ASIA,
SPEAKS THE LANGUAGE,
GROWS UP TO BE
A MIDDLE-CLASS WHITE GUY
IN MONTANA AND
OVER A PERIOD OF YEARS
INADVERTANTLY WRITES
A FEW POEMS
FROM THIS
LIMITED PERSPECTIVE

Do the Math

I'm just goin' as far as the Wye, if that'll help

I'm goin' to Arlee

You'll be closer, get in if you want

He slams the truck's door against a gusting wind
and slides in
My worn-smooth, lined leather work gloves
lay between us
palms up, curled open
as if
for alms

The old Chevy's heater rages
loud white noise
but you can talk over it

You work in town?

No came for the weekend, stayed at my girlfriend's, car died
radiator's shot

Damn, it's so cold, things break when it gets like this
I heard it's real cold all week

300 bucks for a new radiator, shit
Gotta get back to work, I'm late again, my brother's gonna be pissed

Thin torn jeans, shabby Seahawks jacket, black hat
pulled down low
early 20's, 3-day chin scruff, acne scars, reservation accent

chapped red hands
I added these things up
and now you do too
Can we even help but do such math?

Would he make calculations of me, my old truck
stained coveralls
weathered expensive boots
what would the sum be?

Or was he thinking about better chances at the Wye truck stop
the blistering wind
his brother's impatience, late for work again
the dead 90's Honda marooned on a shitty trailer park street
augured into frozen snow and gravel
where there should have been a sidewalk
Or maybe, just his stinging hands
about to be burning cold
again

He stared straight into the windshield
hunched forward
as if he was already back in the spiraling snow, icy wind

Turning into the truck stop at the Wye
I tried out some possible sentences
in the silence of my head
"Hey its cold, take these
I've got two more pairs at home just like'em"
"You'll need these, I've got others"
or "Here, you want 'em?"

We pulled up and he was out, too quick
for me to choose
what to say

Leaders to the Promised Land

We flew past the Washington monument in an Uber
just after midnight
It shined like a sword rising from the earth
You could almost hear the ground breaking beside it as it rose
We banked a curve at speed
and caught a view of the Jefferson memorial
Beams of eternal light
addressed it from below, in cathedral-like glory

What these guys set in motion became
airports, freeway Uber rides, buildings and buildings
and people everywhere
coast to coast
A few weeks earlier a famous writer spoke right into my ears
through little pieces of plastic
like I was the only one listening, but it was
for anyone
His words boomeranged back into my head right then
while we rocketed down
that empty
multi-lane highway
passing
so much majesticness

Their ideas were timeless
and
slavery was no side hustle for these dudes, it was their main gig
it was
how they made their money

Beautiful, isn't it?
Said the driver, in a thick accent
I heard central America

Yeah. It is. Have you had a busy night?

We chatted like that till we glided into the turn-around
of a sprawling muscular hotel
It ate the whole block and a hillside, soaring into the night sky

Contactless check-in, I had no front-desk instructions
as to where to go
so wandered looking for signage guidance
till I ran into a security guard standing by a bank of sleeping
elevators

Yes, yes, It's kind of confusing
his eyes smiled, above his mask
His voice said Nigeria, but that's a best guess
He started to explain — curves, rights and lefts
stairs and elevators
floors named
but not numbered
then he said

Just follow me, it's no problem, I'll show you

And he led the way

Hana

Our rental car crawls around neck-jarring corners
pulls against gravity
up up up the all curves Hana road
Again and again
we cross one-lane stone bridges
cut under
jungle trees hanging at janky angles
Water
weeps in sheets from the mossy rock wall holding back
the sopping forest
falls into stone cataracts carved against the road's shoulder
runs
in culverts under us
gushes
toward the ocean thousands of feet below

On the west side of the island
we left haolies of every shape and size, from lobster pink
to nut brown
every shade of white
We turned away from luxury hotels
taco trucks
and the occasional celebrity sighting
to head up this road

Driving sea-sick into Hana we pass a diabetes info billboard
a food pantry
a free clinic
a few honor system roadside fruit stands
This feels more like a reservation town than a tourist trap
We stay for a week

Early morning on our last day
at the far edge of this hardscrabble place
behind a Japanese hardware store sided in rusted roofing
I separate our vacation's
glass, paper, newspaper, plastic
into fermenting dumpsters
Across the empty lot
a local in a tank top takes a long look at me
A bull's shoulders cut down from his linebacker neck
His bad-ass shaved head gleams
in the fresh morning light
The words "East Side" twitch
in cursive green ink across a grapefruit size bicep
as he flip-flops, board shorts
slow walks
towards me

I can see him ingest the tourist irony that I am
Yep, he knows I know
my soft pale presence here commodifies the last sliver of real
this island's got
He walks at me
We're the only people in the lot

My haolie-ness shines like a beacon
In that moment everything else I believe I am
melts
like ice on the pavement
From Dole's thievery of the archipelago to the pearl chain of
resorts and golf courses
to coconuts for sale at every beach-side pull out
Whitey won, took it all
and now this last piece, this crummy little town too?

Hey man
He says
Thanks for recycling

POEMS TO

To Kim in Fall

Orange, yellow, striped in kelly green
or dark as jade
Delicata, Kubocha, Sunshine, Carnival, Sweet Dumpling, Buttercup
winter squash
You clipped, lifted, and placed each one
into 3' totes on pallets
stems up, stems down
locked in
so they won't bounce and cut each other on the tractor ride back
pallet after pallet

Sorting
with a ruthless eye
and the unsentimental professional gentleness of a nurse
you roll them in your hands
fill 40 lb. boxes
for Bob, Scott, The Ranch, the Growers Co-op
but you cull the ones with rotted spots, too much mouse chew
they'll get cooked soon
or given away
and some head to our cooler for the winter
then the counter and the oven
months from now

That we could all be so swift and careful
thorough as an accountant, steady as a gem cutter, decisive
as a judge
Your squash shines back to the world
you
Each one, just right

To the Mayor

(JOHN ENGEN PASSED AWAY A FEW MONTHS AFTER THIS WAS WRITTEN)

The animal shelter advocate's voice cracked, her hands
slashed the air, swordfight style
She came looking for dollars, a support letter for a grant
The situation was dire, and right now
Cats
feral as raccoons, proliferating like rabbits
Her voice picked up the pace, she sprinted into the last leg of
her 440-yard pitch
Telling her story staccato
words popped like strings of little firecrackers

Trap, sterilize, release, grant funding, in-kind match, shelter space
volunteers, the community

Faster now

Shelter space, volunteers, grants, the community, in-kind match
letter of support

Faster yet, and she stumbled over the finish line

Trap, Sterilize, Euthanize

Then quiet

Her last words echoed around in the conference room
bounced off the fake-wood table
the anonymous art, the wide window onto the grey street
and hung in the air

Trap, Sterilize, Euthanize

Your eyes squinted a bit, your voice took on
the gravity of a judge
the kindness of a teacher

Don't you think that's a little extreme?

I think to you, replay this scene
and laugh
It works whenever I do it, whenever I need to
Nearly everyone I know
has a story like this
of you

So, I have an offer for the universe, for you
As I am the same age, and have lived a life of family, land, labor
snow and sun
mountains, coulees, and friends
Riches all
How about you give me some
of your pain?

Trouble is, all those other people, with their stories
will want in on the deal
Even as sick as you are, there might not be enough
to go around

To Laurie in Panama, Idaho, NYC, Somewhere Far From Here

If you were here
we would settle in to pick strawberries as fast as we could
it would go like this:

So many strawberries, and only an hour left
in our harvest morning
Your hands flash through foliage, eyes darting between
your teenage charges and me
across from you
I'd launch into last night's dinner and how it went down

Visiting older daughter ran the show:
chop broccoli, she said — use the stems too, cut them long and thin

Yes, and I'll grab some garlic scapes

*And we'll need lime, fish sauce and the dark soy sauce
cilantro from the field, scallions from the cooler — for condiments,
and a romaine
for salad*

I'll get the noodles going, and make the sauce

Still at home younger daughter stayed out of the fray
made dessert
Mini strawberry shortcakes
The two bantered
jabbed and joked at each other
I stayed quiet, better to soak up their presence

I would gush about this, in the strawberries with you
Walk through the process of making pad see – oow, the desert
the dressing
and you would affirm, so good so good
look me right in the eye and tell me what I know
How dreamy to cook
with my nearly grown daughters
that this is as good as making dinner gets

But you are at least one great state away now
maybe a continent, and certainly
more than a year
new job, new town, new life

I think of talking through all this with you in the berries
But the you I have in my head
the you I would trust with stories of daughters
and cooking
that you holds fast in time, unchanged
While the real you
roasts broccoli for people I've never met
bikes through a landscape I don't know
makes a new life

If I could I surely would
harvest these berries with you at speed, to learn
the you now

To Khun Vim

My friend Vim
sits
in the early morning, open-air, breakfast light, of a Thai guest house
circa 1990

Head down
a shock of mid-western wheat blonde hair flops
across his forehead
hiding one eye at a punk rock slant
A loose, pale blue oxford
untucked, first two buttons open, sleeves rolled up
hangs heavy with humidity
onto baggy linen shorts
Legs crossed, one flip-flop hinges in the air
a cloth shoulder bag hangs over the back of the chair
steam rises from his coffee

Folded at the spine, Harpers, The Atlantic
The Christian Science Monitor or
maybe yesterday's Herald Tribune
lays before him

He had a nanny in Holland
Lived in rural Illinois for a while before
prepping at St. Paul's
studied poly-sci at Bowdoin
and then the Peace Corps, we were there together

First time we met
second day of our pre-departure orientation
in an anywhere-America-upscale-business hotel lobby

he looked up from his paper
lifted
the corner of his smile

X is playing tonight
A question statement masked as a possible new friend cultural test

He played They Might Be Giants in his room
quoted The Graduate
set a chair inside the door of his Thai house so he could sit
while taking off his teacher shoes
bantered clichés with me
like tennis volleys

That's an entirely different kettle of fish

Yeah, we'd better run it up the flagpole, see how it flies

Hey if it walks like a duck...

Well, the shoe does fit

I can see him, clear as I can see the sooty Thai street before me now
straining to swat a verbal return without
breaking into a head-back, round mouthed, seal bark laugh

Almost 30 years gone, back here again
Harpers in my left hand, folded back against its spine
steam rising from a hot cup
in the brief early morning coolness of this outdoor
Chiang Mai hotel lobby
I drift
from the crisp prose before me, and think
to him

To Steve, A Lifetime Ago

Bare feet slap wet Asian sand
chasing
an orange disc
floating against a cobalt sky
Ropey salt-water wet hair bounced on my neck
to the rhythm of racing footfalls

Running headlong
eyes
to the sky
running
like a cliff diver falls in the night
blind, by choice
One arm reaching, fingers extended
To meet, at speed, a falling orange circle
in perfect
running step union
Catch
then jog out the sprint, a denouement to the drama
stop, spin
and whip it back
to you

To Danny Baum

You and I drive up the Blackfoot in the dark, hike in
before shooting light
field dress a buck by mid-morning
We bone it out right there, pack the meat in bags
load up and go, no fuss
in and out
Iron sites on your WW1 gun
you scoff at scopes, heavy drags
At the picnic table in the yard between your alley house
and the big house
a few blocks from downtown
we finish butchering by late afternoon
Golden leaves crunching under foot, golden November light
all around
Rabbi, you say
you do realize how good we've got it, don't you?

———

Three-year old Quinn, squawks to you, really draws it out
I wanna be the blue frog
Rosa says I can't
You ask him if he can say "no" in a whining, plaintive voice

Noooooo, he says

———

When a deep grey February cough knocks me down
you speculate on accessing the National Strategic Reserve
of hot and sour soup
You show me how to cook the poor man's frittata
stove top, then broil
hand me a cutting board and say
You are the Special Undersecretary of finely slicing onions
and then make Kim
the North American Bureau Chief of Topping Green Beans

Walking back from downtown, I fret
about squandering my little money on a deli sandwich
I'm a cancer survivor, you say, *if you see something you want, just get it*
next month could be
game over

You hand me a diaper bag, and hold Georgia, swaddled and
bundled for the trip
We stand in a cloud of airport noise
people coming and going past us, at speed
You kiss her head, wrap her
in you
Rock, sob
and hand her to me, to return to a birth mother
who changed her mind
I turn away
to walk to the gate, knowing you watch us
disappear

Kim and I lived in a few hundred square feet, paid rent
with farmers market money
I came into your alley house dripping
in a cloud of steam and a towel, swelling with luxury borrowed
from the Academic's big house
You look out the window
then back at me
I've been wondering about your last name, is it from the Aramaic,
"too lazy to close the hot tub", or the Sephardic, "too forgetful to close
the hot tub?"

———

After the accident with my baby daughter
fine, but hurt, my fault
You came looking, and found me
planting winter squash starts on my knees in the rain
tears dropping off my cheeks
What the fuck are you doing, you say, pulled me up
hugged me
for a long time

———

You dropped Rosa off and as you drove away, I saw the words
you finger carved into the May morning frost
on the side of our hoophouse
"Big Ag Sucks"
You slow, before turning out of the driveway
lean out the window into the icy air
and yell
You left Santa Cruz by choice!

———

Coming to your house one evening
the farmer I looked up to, the builder/performance artist
who everyone talked about
the edgy academic from the big house, and you
fighting insomnia
to make your book deadline
I know everyone well enough and can speak their language
but with all the confidence of
a new kid 8th grader
And you invited me to come for drinks, as if I belonged
with these men of your generation
one notch older
but
miles from me

———

You left decades ago, Mexico, New York, Boulder, Paris
but always called
After a stint in the Obama White House
Rosa's at Harvard Law school
my farming mentor Steve is an old friend, our kids all grown
better than I could have imagined
and your cancer returned angry a few years back

I was at a hotel in a distant place
for work
when Steve called with the news

———

I can still hear your voice

Printed in the USA
CPSIA information can be obtained
at www.ICGtesting.com
LVHW07033513130923
757994LV00002B/379